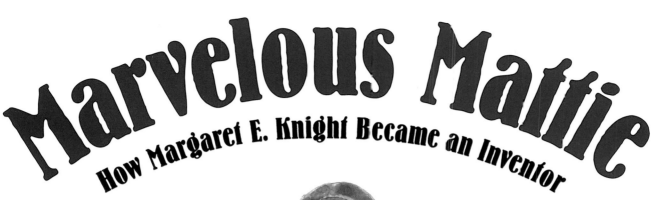

Marvelous Mattie
How Margaret E. Knight Became an Inventor

Emily Arnold McCully

FARRAR STRAUS GIROUX

NEW YORK

Thanks to Rick Randall of the Lowell Machine Shop and to Eileen O'Brien in the library at the Amoskeag Mills, Manchester, New Hampshire.

Distributed in Canada by Douglas & McIntyre Ltd.

Color separations by Chroma Graphics PTE Ltd.

Printed and bound in the United States of America by Phoenix Color Corporation

Designed by Robbin Gourley

First edition, 2006

5   7   9   10   8   6   4

www.fsgkidsbooks.com

Library of Congress Cataloging-in-Publication Data

McCully, Emily Arnold.

Marvelous Mattie : how Margaret E. Knight became an inventor /

Emily Arnold McCully.— 1st ed.

    p. cm.

    ISBN-13: 978-0-374-34810-6

    ISBN-10: 0-374-34810-3

    1. Knight, Margaret E., 1838–1914—Juvenile literature.

[1. Inventors—United States—Biography—Juvenile literature.]

T40.K55 M37 2006

609.2 B 22

2004056415

All black-and-white line drawings are by Emily Arnold McCully except for the patent drawings on page 30.

For Margaret, marvelous editor

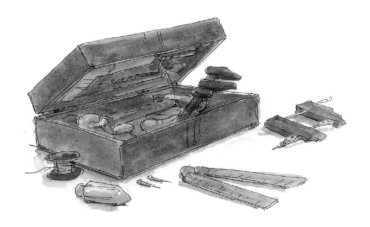

Mattie Knight lived in a little house in York, Maine, with her widowed mother and older brothers, Charlie and Jim. They were poor, but Mattie didn't feel poor. She had inherited her father's toolbox. When she thought of things that could be made with the tools, she drew them in a notebook labeled *My Inventions*. Her brothers called the sketches her brainstorms.

Mattie made a whirligig for Charlie and a jumping jack for Jim. For her mother, who sat up late on cold nights sewing to earn a living, she made a foot warmer.

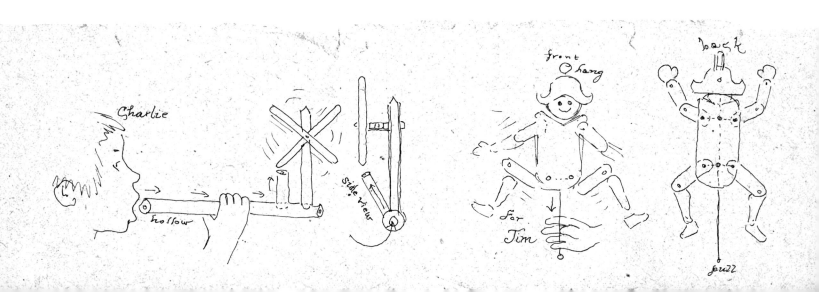

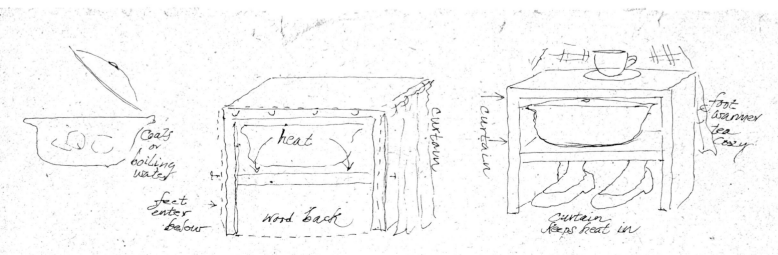

coals or boiling water

feet enter below

heat

Wood back

curtain

curtain keeps heat in

curtain

foot warmer tea cozy

In the spring, Charlie and Jim said, "Won't you make us a special kite?" Mattie sketched a few kites with different shapes and struts. She picked the best one and set to work on it.

"What's Mattie doing now?" their mother asked.

"She's had a brainstorm," the boys said. Their mother shook her head. Mattie was a strange girl, she thought, happiest with her pencil, her jackknife, and her hammer.

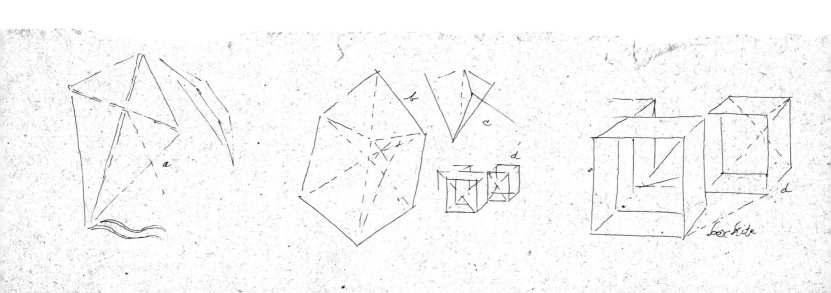

Mattie and the boys took the finished kite to Ward's Hill. Jim ran with it into the wind.

"Faster!" Mattie called. The kite trembled briefly, took a dive, then rose on a sudden gust.

"Yahoo!" Charlie yelled. The kite soared higher and higher.

"Who made that?" some town boys asked.

"Mattie made it."

"She didn't! A girl couldn't make that!"

The following winter, Mattie made sleds for Charlie and Jim, and they won every race down Ward's Hill. Four boys asked Mattie to make sleds for them to race. "It'll cost you a quarter apiece," Mattie said. The boys agreed, and every afternoon after school Mattie worked on the sleds. She gave the money to her mother, but the family was still poor.

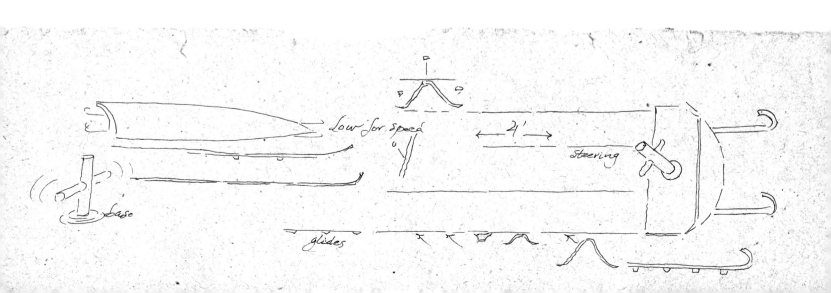

When Mattie was eleven, Mrs. Knight gathered the children together and said, "I've heard there are jobs in the textile mills in Manchester, New Hampshire. The boys and I will work, and Mattie will go to school until she is twelve. The company will rent us a house."

Manchester was a brand-new brick town. With her family gone for thirteen hours every day, Mattie was lonely.

After school, while she waited for them to come home, she liked to explore the complex of mills, but the overseers chased her from the spinning and weaving rooms.

One day, she heard a tremendous roar coming from a building. She went inside and saw that men were building a huge iron machine. Mattie opened her notebook and began to sketch.

"Have you lost your way, little miss?" a man asked.

"This is a machine shop, isn't it?" Mattie replied.

"Well, what does a young girl want here?" he asked.

"I love machines!" Mattie said.

"I guess you must," he replied. "Our shop usually repairs looms, but we've been asked to manufacture this locomotive."

Mattie's eyes glowed. "What's it for?" she asked.

"Why, for the railroad! This is the *General Washington*. It will haul cars on the New York Central lines."

The man's name was Mr. Baldwin, and he answered all her questions. Mattie felt very much at home in the machine shop. She told her family what she'd discovered.

"Whatever can this lead to?" her mother said, sighing.

When Mattie turned twelve, she went to work in the mill, rising with the four-thirty bell in the morning and trudging home to the seven-thirty bell at night. One day, a shuttle shot off the end of a loom and slammed into a girl's head. The injured girl was Rebecca, who lived next door to Mattie's family.

Mattie ran to help. "Out of the way!" the overseer shouted. Rebecca was carried out while the looms clattered on and the other girls tried not to lose their threads. Nothing ever halted production. "Horrible!" someone said. "It's the fault of the machines!"

After work, Mattie walked home with her family. She went over and over the sequence of events that had led to the accident. She pictured the shuttle, what it was supposed to do, and how it had gone wrong. A machine was an invention and could always be improved.

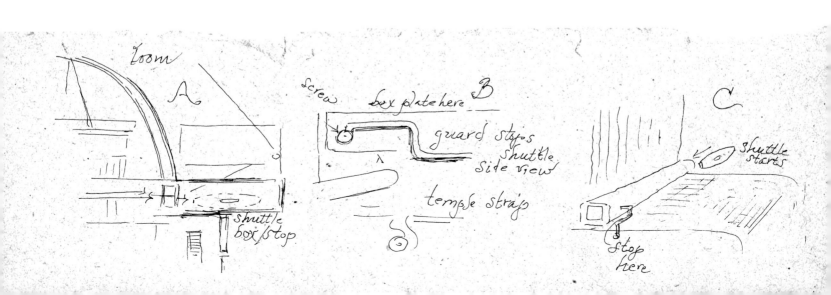

That evening, there was a vigil for Rebecca. A weaver said it wasn't uncommon for threads to snap, making missiles of the shuttles. Mattie sat scribbling in her notebook. Suddenly, an idea took shape. A metal guard attached to the box plate would stop a shuttle that had run off the track. It was simple. If only she could try it out!

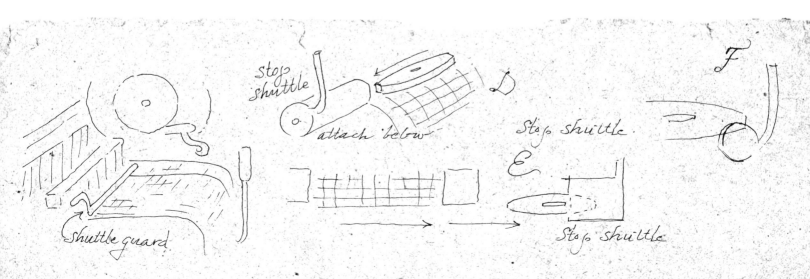

Mattie showed her notebook to Mr. Baldwin. "My goodness! These are the drawings of a real inventor," he said, "and I think your solution is right! I'm going to take it to the boss." The head engineer was impressed and showed Mattie's idea to one of the mill owners. A few weeks passed. Rebecca got better. Then, one day, workmen arrived and began installing metal guards on all the looms in every mill in Manchester.

The guards worked just as Mattie had designed them to do. Never again would someone be hurt by a runaway shuttle.

"Oh, Mattie, I'm so proud of you!" her mother said.

Mr. Baldwin congratulated her. "You ought to own a patent on your idea," he remarked.

"What's a patent?" Mattie asked.

He explained that inventors registered their ideas with the government to protect them from being stolen. Once patented, an idea could be sold or the inventor could manufacture the device herself. "But I guess they wouldn't give a patent to a little girl," he said.

Mattie worked in the mill for a few more years. Cotton prices fell and production slowed. "I want to look for a better opportunity," Mattie told her mother when she turned eighteen.

"I hate to give you up," said her mother, "but I know you must go."

Mattie moved away from home and worked in several different factories. Then, after the Civil War, she heard of a job in Springfield, Massachusetts. It was in a factory that mass-produced paper bags that used to be made by hand. Its machines cut paper from long rolls, then folded and pasted each length shut at the bottom, like an envelope. But the bags didn't stand upright, and grocers had to use one hand to hold them open for filling. Bulky items tended to split the bags.

In Springfield, Mattie shared a room with Sadie, who worked in a shoe factory. Mattie had not been working at the bag factory for very long when a man mentioned that he knew someone who was trying to invent a better machine that could cut and glue a square-bottomed bag. Such a machine would make a far better product. Soon, Mattie heard about others who were trying to invent an improved machine.

Mattie decided she must try to invent one herself. She set up a workshop in the basement of her rooming house and sketched possible improvements on the bag machine. Sadie came downstairs to see what Mattie was up to. "It's bedtime," she said. "Whatever are you doing?"

Mattie made a notation in her notebook before she answered. "Inventing," she said.

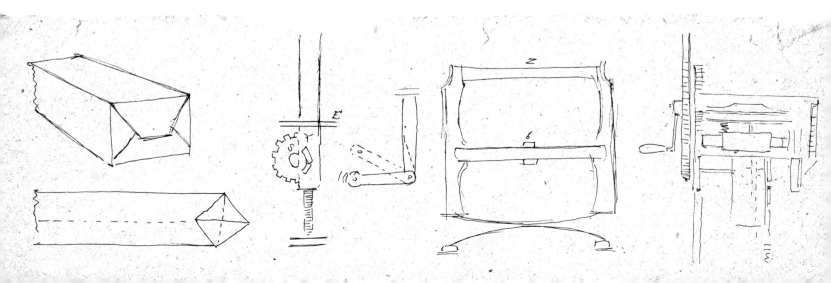

"Well, you're not like any girls I ever knew!" said Sadie. Mattie explained what she was working on. Sadie took to checking up on her new friend. "How is it coming along?"

"We'll see," Mattie would say.

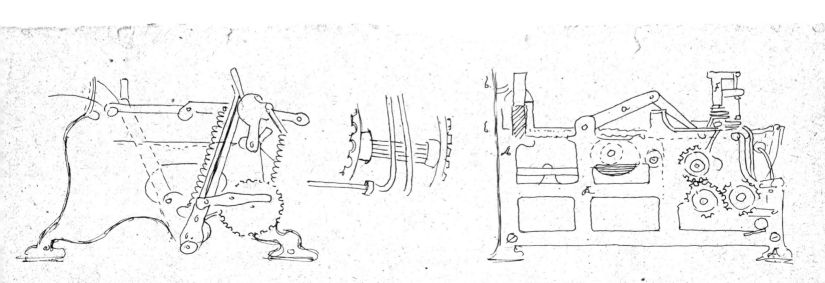

Mattie worked and worked on her bag-making machine. She made paper cut-out versions of her machine, refining the process by trial and error. There was no end to improving, it seemed. But the day came to try making some bags. She built a prototype machine out of wood, using her father's old toolbox.

Would it work? When the first bag rolled out, the paper caught. Mattie found the problem and fixed it. Gingerly, she started the machine again. The roll proceeded smoothly. One after another, paper bags poured from her invention.

Over the next few weeks, she made several thousand bags, each of them with a flat bottom, enabling it to stand upright and hold bulky groceries without ripping.

"You've done it!" Sadie cried.

"I have!" Mattie agreed.

An inventors club had formed in Springfield. Mattie went to a meeting and introduced herself. She told the men she had invented a new machine and wanted to obtain a patent.

"There's an excellent machine shop in Boston," one of the inventors told her. "Have them make an iron prototype to file with the patent office."

When Mattie told Sadie, she said, "You're going to Boston all by yourself?"

"I have to," Mattie replied.

She used some of her savings to rent a room in Boston so that she could supervise the casting and assembly of her machine. "I think you've got a money idea here," the shop foreman said. "But why doesn't your husband come in and see to this himself?"

"I am the inventor," Mattie said. "And you need to recast this part. It doesn't exactly meet my specifications."

One day when she arrived at the shop, a man pushed past her and stormed out the door. At the time, she thought only that he was rude. The prototype took a few weeks longer to complete. It was a moment of triumph when she loaded a roll of paper and proved that her machine produced uniform, square-bottomed bags.

With the help of a friendly machinist, she carried her invention to the patent office and filled out the paperwork. The clerk read it and handed it back to her. "Miss, this has already been patented, only last week." Mattie gazed in bewilderment at the record. Indeed, one Charles F. Annan had submitted a prototype and filed a patent for an identical invention.

"That's the fellow who was in our shop," said the machinist. "He's stolen your idea!"

Mattie had never felt so discouraged.

The clerk said, "This looks like a matter for the court."

"The court?" Mattie asked.

"If you can prove to the judge that this idea is yours, you get the patent."

Mattie had to hire a lawyer. It took the rest of her savings. "Do you have a notebook?" he asked. Mattie said that she had. The lawyer told her to bring Sadie to testify. Mattie had to go to Springfield and persuade Sadie to come to Boston.

Mr. Annan took the stand. He told the judge that the invention was obviously his, because "Miss Knight could not possibly understand the mechanical complexities of the machine."

When Sadie took the stand, she was so frightened she spoke in a whisper. "This woman is even less competent than Miss Knight," snorted Charles Annan. Mattie's lawyer asked Sadie if she ever saw Mattie work on her invention. "Oh yes," whispered Sadie. "When?" asked the lawyer. "Every night for two years," Sadie told him.

Then Mattie's lawyer asked her to show the court her drawings, her paper patterns, and the notebook with all of its entries. The judge pored over them.

"I must compliment you on the entire originality of this machine," he said finally. "This evidence and the testimony of the witness prove Miss Knight's priority of invention. Mr. Annan shall be forever disgraced in history."

Mattie beamed and Sadie gave a little cheer.

Drawings from an 1871 patent showing views of Margaret Knight's paper-bag machine.

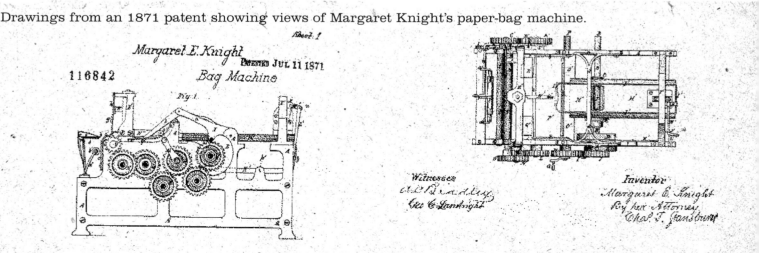

The representative of a manufacturing firm was on hand for the verdict. He offered Mattie $50,000 if she would sell him her invention outright. Mattie didn't hesitate. "No, thank you," she said. "I intend to go into business for myself."

She improved the bag machine and applied for another patent. Then she set up the Eastern Paper Bag Company with a business partner. Mattie was a professional inventor for the rest of her life. When she died at the age of seventy-six, her obituary referred to her as "the Lady Edison."

People still use the paper bags from Mattie's invention every day.

Author's Note

During Margaret E. Knight's lifetime, from 1838 until 1914, the industrial revolution, American expansionism, and the national go-ahead spirit spawned both an unprecedented wave of invention and restrictions on respectable women, who were supposed to devote themselves to the domestic sphere. Mattie was dogged all her life by the belief that women's brains were inadequate for inventing. By becoming not only an inventor but a professional one, with twenty-two patents to her credit and over ninety original inventions, Mattie both defied and exemplified her times. Her elementary school education didn't hold her back, for she had just the contriving, exploring, visualizing, ingenious, persistent mind required by her work. She could think up an idea and figure out how to execute it without necessarily understanding the theory that explained it. From the time she was exposed to the machine shop in Manchester, she imagined mechanical concepts that allowed for alternative combinations or improvements.

The December 2, 1872, issue of *Woman's Journal* ran an article that gives us some firsthand insight into Mattie's views about her childhood: "Miss KNIGHT of Boston has invented a machine for making paper bags, and is having a number of them manufactured at Chicopee, under her own supervision. The workmen employed were at first sceptical as to her mechanical ability; but she cured them of this by going daily, and working among them,—detecting mistakes, and improving plans, with a keener eye than any man in the works . . . She said [of her abilities]: 'It is only following out nature. As a child, I never cared for things that girls usually do . . . My friends were horrified. I was called a tomboy; but that made very little impression on me. I sighed sometimes, because I was not like other girls; but wisely concluded that I couldn't help it, and sought further consolation from my tools . . . I'm only sorry I couldn't have had as good a chance as a boy, and have been put to my trade regularly.'"

Having to improvise a career, Mattie never got rich, but tackled, among other things, window sashes and automobile engines as well as paper bags. The exact nature of her loom safety device, invented when she was twelve, remains something of a mystery. In a *New York Times* article from 1913 she referred to it as a "shuttle cover." Historians usually assert that it was either a "shuttle restraining device" or a "stop action device." Unfortunately, nobody seems to really know what her device was or how it worked, and no records of it have come to light.

Bibliography

MacDonald, Ann L. *Women Inventors*. New York: Ballantine Books, 1992.

Petroski, Henry. *Small Things Considered*. New York: Alfred A. Knopf, 2003.

Petrusso, Annette. "Margaret E. Knight." In *Notable Women Scientists*, ed. Pamela Proffitt. Detroit: The Gale Group, 1999. P. 294.

Stanley, Autumn. *Mothers and Daughters of Invention*. Metuchen, N.J.: Scarecrow Press, 1993.